Ethel

HEAVEN AND MIRTH®

David

and Bubblebath-Sheba

AND
OTHER BIBLE STORIES TO TICKLE YOUR SOUL

by Mike Thaler

Illustrated by Dennis Adler

*Equipping Kids
for Life*

A Faith Parenting Guide can be found on page 32.

For Clyde Van Cleve,
who makes these books beautiful
by design.
Mike

Faith Kids® is an imprint of
Cook Communications, Colorado Springs, Colorado 80918
Cook Communications, Paris, Ontario
Kingsway Communications, Eastbourne, England

DAVID AND BUBBLEBATH-SHEBA
© 2000 by Mike Thaler for text and Dennis Adler for illustrations

Published in association with the literary agency of Alive Communications, Inc.,
7680 Goddard St., Suite 200, Colorado Springs CO 80920.

Edited by Jeannie Harmon
Design by Clyde Van Cleve

First hardcover printing, 2000
Printed in Singapore
04 03 02 01 00   5 4 3 2 1

ISBN: 0-78143-511-0

Letter from the Author

Taking this opportunity, I would like to share with you how this book came about. Born sixty-two years ago, I have been a secular children's book author most of my life. I was also content to have a fast-food relationship with God from the drive-by window. At the age of sixty, I came into the banquet by inviting Jesus Christ into my heart. Since then my life has been a glorious feast. These stories are part of that celebration.

One night I sat and watched a sincere grandfather trying to read Bible stories to his squirming grandchildren. I asked him, "Aren't there any humorous retellings of Bible stories that are vivid and alive for kids?" He rolled his eyes and said, "This is it." The kids rolled their eyes too.

This made me sad, for the Bible is the most exciting, valuable, and alive book I know—as is its Author. So I went into my room, with this in mind, and wrote "Noah's Rainbow."

Since then God has anointed me with sixty stories that fire my imagination and light up my heart. They are stories which, I hope, are filled with the joy, love, and spirit of the Lord.

Mike Thaler
West Linn 1998

Nuggets from Goldie the miner prophet:
"It's Never Too Late to Eat Right."

Author's Note

I have conscientiously tried to follow each story in word and spirit as found in the Bible. But in some cases, for the sake of storytelling, I have taken minor liberties and added small details. I pray for your understanding in these instances.

Jacob Wrestles with God

The Main Event

J ACOB BELONGED to the WWF★ and the HWF.★★ He was known as Jacob, the Not-So-Hairy. He had a big match coming up, so he sent his family and servants across the river.

★World Wrestling Federation
★★Heaven Wrestling Federation

Then he stepped into the ring
to meet the Mystery Challenger,
who wore purple tights,
a blue mask, and pink sneakers.

They wrestled all night,
but neither could gain
an advantage.
The Mystery Challenger
tried everything;
full nelsons, half nelsons,
eighth nelsons, hammer locks,
ham and lox, lox and bagels,
but Jacob was too hip to get pinned.
So finally the Mystery Challenger
tried the "sock it to me" hold,
but Jacob wouldn't let go.

"Hey, come on. It's morning.
I've got to get back to heaven."

"Not until you bless me,"
said Jacob.

"You didn't sneeze,"
said the Mystery Challenger.
"What's your name?"

"Jacob, the Not-So-Hairy,"

"Well, from now on your name is *Israel*
because you've wrestled with God
and with men, and *is real* hard to beat you."

"What's your name?" asked Jacob.

"My name is Mystery," said the stranger.

"Miss Terry?" asked Jacob.

"No, no," said the stranger,
"Bless you... bye!"
And he disappeared.

So Jacob limped away
and named that spot "the face of God"
because he met God face to face
and lasted 120 rounds,
although he really felt burned out
after the match.

THE END

Nuggets from Goldie, the miner prophet:
"When God loves you, He'll try to pin you."

For the real story, read Genesis 32:22-32.

David and Bubblebath-Sheba

IN THE SPRING,
when robins sing
and kings go off to war,
David thought he'd take
a little break
and sniff the flowers.
So he sent Joab, his general,
out with his army to
capture a few cities
and destroy a few kingdoms.

One night, he went up
on the roof with his telescope
to look at the stars.
But he accidentally adjusted it a little low,
and saw a very beautiful woman across the street
taking a bubble bath.

She also had a rubber duck
and two tugboats
in the tub with her.

"Wow!" exclaimed David,
"two tubboats! I must
know who this woman is!"
He asked his wise man
who knew everyone
in the neighborhood.

"Her name is Bath-Sheba
because she takes a lot of baths.
Unfortunately, she's married,
but she has a single sister
whose name is Shower-Sheba."

"Who's her husband?"
asked David.

"His name is Uriah.
He's a commander
in your army."

"Get me his service record,"
commanded the king.

"Hmm," said David, leafing through it.
"He's honorable, heroic, and handsome."

"That's a lot of H's," said the wise man.

"Send for him," commanded the king.
So Uriah was brought before the king.

"How's Joab and the troops?
How's the war going?"

"Everyone's fine," said Uriah.
"A few guys have spears through their
heads, but besides that, everyone's OK."

"Good," said the king.
"Take a little time off, go home, take a bath."

"I can't, sire, the bathroom is always taken.
My wife washes a lot.
She's a real tub tourist."

"I know—I mean, go," said the king.
But Uriah didn't go home.
He slept on the steps in front of the palace.

"Why didn't you go home?"
asked David the next morning.
"You just live across the street."

"My troops are all sleeping out in the desert.
It wouldn't be fair if I slept in my bed," said Uriah.

"All right, Uriah, return to your troops,
and give this letter to Joab."

Uriah bowed and left for the war.
It would be the last letter
he would ever deliver.
For it instructed Joab
to put Uriah in front
of the worst fighting
and then desert him.

So Uriah
was ordered to charge;
then everyone in back
of him retreated.
When they found him
the next day,
he had the world's
biggest arrow collection.
The news quickly reached David.

"Give him a funeral with full military honors," said David.
"Then invite Bath-Sheba over to use the royal bathtub,
and fill it with a whole fleet of tugs and a flock of rubber ducks."

After an appropriate time of mourning —
about a day and a half — he and Bath-Sheba were married.

But Nathan the prophet
    wouldn't be best man,
        for God was angry at what David had done.

"**Heaven knows,**
I gave him enough wives," said God,
"**now he's really in hot water. Go, Nathan,**
and tell him I'm very annoyed."

So Nathan went to David and told him a story.

    "Once upon a time there was a very rich man
        who had many, many sheep.
        And there was a poor girl named Mary,
    who had only one little lamb.
    Its fleece was white as snow,
        and everywhere that Mary went
    the lamb was sure to go.
    Well, anyway, the rich man
    had important visitors.
    But instead of butchering
    one of his many sheep
    for dinner, he slaughtered
    Mary's little lamb."

"What a rotten guy,"
    shouted David, jumping up.

"He deserves to die."

"Well, my king, you are that guy.
  You killed Uriah who was honorable,
  heroic, and handsome.
   Then you took his wife for your own.
  God is very angry with you.
  Calamity will surely fall on your house.
  You are going to lose all your wives,
  your new infant will not live,
  and you are going to break out with acne."

"Oh, Lord, I have sinned.
  I don't mind losing my wives,
  I don't even mind zits, but Lord,
please spare my baby."

"I have spoken!" said God,
  and Nathan left.
  Soon after,
  David's new son fell very ill
  and David fell on the ground.
  He prayed and fasted,
  but after seven days
  the child died.
  David accepted God's will.

So he got up, kicked Bath-Sheba out of the tub,
  washed his hair, and they went out to a good Persian restaurant.

Nine months later Bath-Sheba gave birth to another son. They named him Solomon.

"He looks like a smart kid," said God. **"I'll be his Godfather, and someday he will rule over Israel."**

In time, the rest of Nathan's prophecy came true.

All of David's wives filed for divorce, and he broke out with many pimples, so that much of his treasury was spent paying alimony and buying Clearasil.

THE END

P.S. Bath-Sheba eventually grew very wrinkled from staying in the tub so long.

Nuggets from Goldie, the miner prophet:
"Soap can clean up your skin, but not your sin."

For the real story, read 2 Samuel 11—12:25.

16

Solomon
Half a Kid
Is Better Than None

OUT OF ALL HIS CHILDREN,
King David picked Solomon
to succeed him.
Adonijah,★ his oldest son,
didn't take it lying down,
until Solomon killed him.
Then he did.

When God asked Solomon
what he'd like the most:
a new Ferrari,
a crown from Tiffany's,
a season ticket to
Yankee Stadium ? ...

Solomon answered, "Wisdom."

★pronounced "I-don'-need-ya."

"Wise choice," said God.
"The tin man wanted a *heart,*
the lion wanted *courage,*
and you want *wisdom.*
What you really need,"
said God, "is a beard."

So God gave Solomon
a big curly beard
which made him
the wisest king of all time.
As a ruler, he not only
measured up to his dad,
but surpassed him.
He made wise decisions every day.
He chose to eat Egg Beaters for breakfast.
He chose not to smoke, and he always
chose to buckle up when he drove his chariot.
But the wisest decision he ever made
involved two women
who both claimed the same baby.

"He's mine," said the first woman.

"Mine," said the second.

"Hold it," said Solomon.
"I'll just cut the baby in two,
and you each can take home half."

"Fine," said the first,
    "but I get the top half."

    "No!" cried the second.
      "Give her the whole baby!"

    By this response,
     Solomon knew
      that the second woman
       was truly the mom,
        so he gave her the whole kid
        and put the first woman
        up for adoption.

    When the people of Israel
    heard of his wise decision,
    they knew their king
    was truly a smart cookie.

  "What do you expect?"
they all exclaimed.
"Just look at his beard!"

THE END

Nuggets from Goldie, the miner prophet:
"The smartest thing you can ever do is love God!"

For the real story, read 1 Kings 3:16–28.

Uzziah Meets the No-Nonsense God

UZZIAH BECAME THE KING OF JUDAH when he was sixteen years old. He was a local boy from Jerusalem, and he did right in the eyes of the Lord. He attended Hebrew school and had a very nice Bar Mitzvah.

So God upheld him
and gave him great success.
He got into the college of his choice,
he was able to get his dad's chariot
every Friday night,
and his fields and vineyards prospered.
He easily defeated all his enemies,
and his army had the sharpest uniforms
and spears that money could buy.
He also invented a small machine gun
which he named after himself—
the *Uzzi*.★

So what happened to him,
you may ask?
Did he live happily ever after?
He could have,
but I'm afraid he didn't.
As he grew more powerful,
he got too big for his crown
and broke God's laws.
He entered the holiest place
in the temple, the room that said
Employees Only, and insisted
on burning incense to the Lord.

★ Only kidding!

All the priests confronted him
and said, "Get outta here!"

But Uzziah, who had
  his censer in hand,
  ready to burn incense,
    didn't have the sense to leave.
    He became incensed,
      which was totally insensitive of him,
    and shouted at the priests
  that he would not be censored.

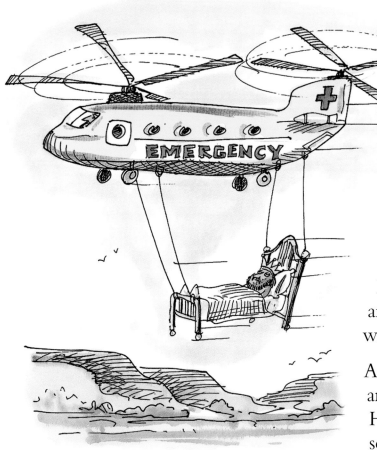

God didn't like
this nonsense,
and while Uzziah
was causing a sensation
in front of God's altar,
the king broke out
with leprosy.
He quickly changed his tune,
and they rushed him
to the emergency room.
But no one could cure him,
and he lived the rest of his life
with a spotty reputation.

As a leper, he wasn't invited to parties,
and he couldn't use public bathrooms.
He had to go on sick leave,
so his son, Jotham,
ran the government.
Uzziah died alone
and miserable.

And on his tombstone, it said:

His Pride

Stopped Him

from Being

the Pride

of God.

THE END

Nuggets from Goldie, the miner prophet:
"If you don't keep your nose clean, you may blow it!"

For the real story, read 2 Chronicles 26.

Balaam
Pin This Tale on the Donkey

BALAAM WAS A PROPHET.
But to make ends meet, he would cast spells and curses
and read fortunes. He had a pretty good reputation.

So when Balak, son of Flipper,
and king of Moab,
looked out his window
and saw the Israelites
camped on his doorstep,
he grew really fearful.

Balak had heard
that they had bashed
the king of Bashan,
mashed the people
of Chemosh, and trashed
the land of Heshbon.

He immediately sent for Balaam to *bail 'im* out
by putting a curse on this rough–and–tumble tribe.

But when Balaam asked God for the curse, God answered, **"No way, José. These folks are My people, the home team, and you should be rooting for them too."**

So Balaam told Balak what God had said.

"Go back to God and ask Him for just a little curse," pleaded Balak, "maybe that their sandals will come undone in the middle of the battle." So Balaam went back to God and asked Him for just a little curse.

"Go with them," said God, **"and I'll think about it."** But God was angry.

Balaam was a pest, and a pest for the wrong side. God sent his angel of death to kill Balaam. When Balaam's donkey, whose name was Ho-Dee,★ saw the angel standing with his silver sword, he jumped off the road.

"Get back on the road," shouted Balaam, and he kicked Ho-Dee hard.

Then the donkey saw the angel standing in the field so he pressed up against a wall.

★Donkey–Ho-Dee (get it?)

"Whoa-Dee, Ho-Dee!" yelled Balaam,
"are ya trying to kill me?"
And he kicked the animal even harder.

Then the donkey saw the angel standing
right in front of them,
so he just sat down.

"This is too much," cried Balaam.
"If I had a sword, you'd be donkey burgers."

Then to Balaam's surprise the donkey spoke.
"Am I not your old buddy Ho-Dee
who has carried you many a mile?
Have I ever acted like this before?"

Balaam thought for a minute.
"No, I can't say that you have."

Then Balaam saw the angel with his sword drawn
and he kicked himself.

"You *better* kick yourself," said the angel.
"You messed up *big time*.
Your donkey's got more horse sense than you."

"What can I do?" cried Balaam.

"Quit wailin', Balaam," said the angel. "Go with Balak,
and do what God tells you to do."

So Balaam went with Balak who built seven altars
and sacrificed four calling birds, three French hens,
two turtle doves, and a partridge in a pear tree.

"Now," said Balak, "give me a real curse
on those Israelites,
and I'll fix it so you
never have to work again."

Balaam got the word from God
and gave it to Balak.

**"The Israelites are
My chosen people.
You don't stand a chance
against them, so before
you go to battle, be sure
your insurance is all paid up."**

"This is not what I wanted to hear," said
Balak. And he built seven more altars
and sacrificed five golden rings.
"Now go back and try again."

This time God was very clear.

**"The odds in heaven are a hundred to one
that you won't be at your next birthday party."**

This did not make Balak happy
because he loved birthday parties, especially his own.

So he built seven more altars and was about to sacrifice seven maids-a-milking when God spoke.

"Look, I am the God who tells it like it is. I don't change My mind and I don't beat around the bush, unless it's burning. Just accept the fact that there's no way you're going to win this battle, and you'd be better off joining the peace corps."

Balak grew angry. "This is not why I hired you. You have not cursed the Israelites, you have not given me and my troops a real good pep talk, so you're fired as of today."

"It's cool," said Balaam.
"I'm going to get my donkey out of here and head for home. But here's a bit of free advice. Don't start reading a book over twenty pages."

THE END

Nuggets from Goldie, the miner prophet:
"God stands by His Word and His people."

For the real story, read Numbers 22–24

HEAVEN AND MIRTH®

David and Bubblebath Sheba

Age: 6 and up

Life Issue:
Obeying God brings positive results.

Spiritual Building Block:
Obedience

Learning Styles

Help your child learn about obedience in the following ways:

Sight: Look up one or more of the stories in a children's version of the Bible. Read the story aloud. Did the main character (Jacob, David, Solomon, Uzziah, or Balaam) obey God? What did he do? God sees everything we do. We cannot hide our actions from Him. But He will give us the strength to make right choices, if we ask His help. Pray with your child, asking God's help for daily choices.

Sound: What are ways that people in these stories disobeyed God? Sometiimes when we take our eyes off of the Lord, we are tempted to do things that don't please Him. What are ways that we disobey God with our actions? by the words we say? Where can we discover what God wants us to do?

Touch: Choose a story to act out. Use other family members to play the additional characters needed. The story of Balaam and his donkey might be fun because your child can add donkey sounds throughout the story. Practice a few times and then have another family member videotape the performance.